Contents

KU-513-058

My name is Michael   4

My mum and dad   6

My sister and brother   8

Playing together   10

Arguing   12

Granny and grandad   14

My uncles and aunts   16

My cousins   18

Cousins far away   20

I love my family   22

Word bank   24

My name is Michael and this is my family.

My dad works in an office.

My mum runs
a shop.

I've got a big sister
and a little brother.

9

Sometimes
we play
together.

11

Sometimes we argue.

12

My granny and grandad often come to stay.

15

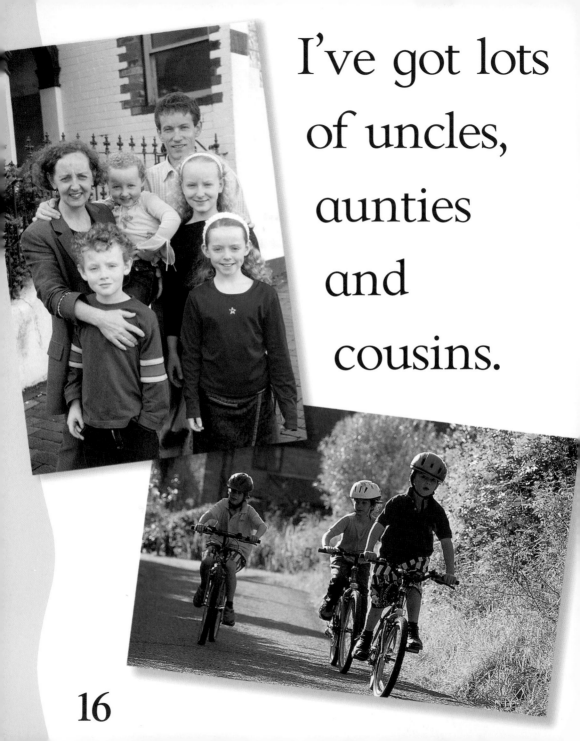

I've got lots of uncles, aunties and cousins.

Some of my cousins live nearby.

Some of my cousins
live a long way away.

I love my family.

Word bank

Look back for these words and pictures.

Aunties

Brother

Cousins

Dad

Grandad

Granny

Mum

Sister

Uncles